Take Me Home

Bethany Jarmul

BELLE POINT PRESS
Fort Smith, Arkansas

Take Me Home:
A Mini Memoir

Cover image: original, *Violin* (1941)
by Cornelius Christoffels and Edward Jewett
The National Gallery of Art.

Edited by Casie Dodd
Design & typography by Belle Point Press

Belle Point Press, LLC
Fort Smith, Arkansas
bellepointpress.com
editor@bellepointpress.com

Find Belle Point Press
on Facebook, Substack,
and Instagram (@bellepointpress)

Printed in the United States of America

28 27 26 25 24 1 2 3 4 5

ISBN: 978-1-960215-20-8

CHAP12/BPP29

A Note on Truth

Some names and identifying details have been adjusted to protect people's privacy. Dialogue, dates, and the narrative arc of events in my life may not be exact because I am human and fallible. These are pieced together from my memories, which may be different from the memories of others. I've done my best to capture the emotional truth of my story.

Contents

Yellow

Definition:
1. Cowardly
2. The color between green and orange

Synonyms:
Chicken-hearted, craven, fearful, lily-livered, spiritless, spineless, timid, trembling, unheroic

Antonyms:
Brave, courageous, confident, strong, bold

MINERS carried caged canaries into the sooty tunnels deep below the Appalachian Mountains—sacrifices to the gods of labor, money lust, liquid greed. Carbon monoxide kills the canaries first, a call to clear, to flee, to fly away from the hole in the earth, from the noxious fumes and dust that settle into pores, nostrils, alveoli.

The ebony crumbles clung to my father's grandfather's hands, formed a ring around his neck, blackened his lungs, silenced his heart. The exhaustion and daily drudgery broke my mother's grandfather's back, leaving him unable to mine, perhaps preserving his life.

Male canaries develop elaborate songs. Loners by nature, they're more apt to croon when isolated, surrounded by nothingness. Their voices vary—the Spanish Timbrado sings of church bells at noon; the Harz Roller's croon is soft, rolling. Belgian Waterslager's chant is percussive, echoing.

The birds' rapid rate of breathing, little lungs, mighty metabolisms made them perfect air testers. In the deepest darkness they sang, chimed, yodeled, and beat-boxed, belted out bubbling melodies, then—suddenly ceased.

Describe them, miners and canaries, as doomed, ill-fated, damned, as brave, plucky, unflinching, as lemon, amber, golden—anything but *yellow*.

Unto a Place & Its People

I was born at home—in the same bed in which I was conceived, in the tiny West Virginia town where my mother was raised. The rows of small houses interrupted by the peaks and dips of the hills. The Appalachian Mountains in every direction, including underfoot. Deciduous trees line the background and litter the foreground with their verdant buds, mood-ring leaves, or as in the season of my birth—stark nakedness. And like something out of a novel—two traffic lights, a couple local diners, a park where the river runs, the squirrels chatter, the children swing and holler. Parked along the streets, you'd find pick-up trucks, sedans, and minivans—some with rust. In backyards: beagles, golden retrievers, mutts; gardens with green beans, cucumbers, tomatoes; a couple chicken coops, three or four stray cats.

During labor Kathy, my mother, sat on her bed in my parents' rental house, in a long-sleeved cotton nightgown with frilly trim, chatting with her mother-in-law on the phone, twirling the phone's curly cord around her finger.

Ten years prior, in the early '80s, twenty-three-year-old Kathy watched with wide eyes as nurses prepped her pregnant cousin for a C-section. Her cousin's arms were spread wide and strapped down, Jesus-style. Her body—a sacrifice to bring forth new life. After the procedure, Kathy held the baby up so her cousin could stroke the baby's face with her fingers—her arms still restrained.

New to her Christian faith, Kathy told God: "I'm having my future babies at home. You're going to have to bring me a man that is okay with that." Her deepest desire was to be a wife and mother. When she "finally" found such a man, my father, and got married at thirty-one, she quit her teaching job, made baby-making her full-time occupation until motherhood (which as one would imagine didn't take long).

The midwives camped out in the living room with sleeping bags, waiting. Kathy paced up and down the hallway. The sun set. The sun rose. Still, she labored. A dusting of snow outside, resting on the red railing of their deck and lining every blade of grass. After thirty-one hours of unmedicated labor, I arrived the afternoon of February 27, 1992. My dad cut my umbilical cord.

Eight months later, a reporter interviewed my parents about my birth as part of an article entitled "What does a midwife do anyway?" The newspaper included photos of me smiling in my playpen with my Snuggle bear, bunny rattle, and picture books.

My birth cost my parents seven hundred fifty dollars (equivalent to $1,600 today)—a lot of money for them, living off my father's teaching income. "It doesn't matter to me because I got the kind of birth that I wanted," my mom said.

My dad told the reporter: "I think that our country has

made childbirth into an industry. I think that there are many things that are done during the childbirth process that are more medical than natural, that aren't necessary, but are somewhat of a precaution. We believe that the Lord will protect us. We know that he wanted the baby to come out all right."

And there I was, the fulfillment of my mother's dream—a healthy, smiling baby—evidence, certainly in my parents' minds, that my father was right.

Big Feelings, Little Self

Strong emotions activate one's amygdala and hippocampus at almost the same time, like synchronized lightning flashes in the brain—making an emotional event more memorable. My earliest memories are tied to emotions that hit like a sudden thunderstorm—drenching me, frightening me with their power.

1. INDIGNATION

Thunderstorms are the atmosphere's way of releasing pent-up energy. Heat, like anger, grows inside a cumulus cloud, the water molecules wrestling, dancing, fighting, until a thunderstorm is born—rain released, thunderous explosions, accents of electrical wonder.

In a preschool classroom filled with colorful toys, alphabet posters, and tiny chairs, my best friend, Kate, and I play with Sky Dancers, pull their strings, sending the pink-and-purple fairies floating through the air like helicopter seeds. I notice the age level on the box reads "5+." Kate is four.

"You can't play with this toy. It's not for four-year-olds," I say.

"Yes, I can. I play with it all the time."

I march over to Kate's mom. "Kate can't play with this toy. She's only four."

"It's fine. Kate can play with it," Kate's mom says.

"But, but . . . she's not supposed to!"
"It's fine, Bethany. Now, go play."
I stomp back over to Kate, cheeks and ears flushed.

2. ANXIETY

Giant clouds tower on the horizon. The sky darkens to a swirl of charcoal. Wind carries off the warmth, rattling tree branches, littering yards with leaves, soda bottles, cigarette butts. In the distance, thunder rumbles, grumbles. It's coming.

In kindergarten, stern Mrs. Wolfe, with glasses on the tip of her nose, asks each of us, "What is the name of the street where you live?" She goes down the rows of wooden desks, asking each child.

Towheaded David, who is sitting in front of me, says, "West Virginia."

"No, that's our state. What's the name of your street?"

David shakes his head in confusion, shrugs.

My forehead wrinkles into a scowl. My mother taught me a jingle to learn my address. I know it by heart, yet I am sweating.

"Bethany, what's the name of your street?"

"West Virginia," I say.

"No, that's the state."

Panic settles over my small body. My heart hummingbirds.

Kate pipes up to my rescue: "Mrs. Wolfe, that really is the name of Bethany's street: West Virginia Avenue."

"Yes," I say. "West Virginia Avenue. That's what I said."

Mrs. Wolfe offers an affirmative grunt. I hope Kate can read the "thank you" in my eyes.

3. DISAPPOINTMENT

The ground is dry and needy—flowers wilting, grass dying, crops unyielding. Thunder crashes, lightning flashes, but despite the thirst, there is no rain. Called a "dry thunderstorm"—the clouds' rain droplets evaporate into the air before they reach the parched earth.

On Christmas morning 1998, I'm six; my family sits around our dining room table. We sing "Happy Birthday" to Jesus, then blow out the candles on our cinnamon rolls. Dad reads the story of Jesus' birth from the Bible, but I'm restless. Presents wait beneath the tree, and I want a Barbie doll more than anything—one just like Kate's.

When it's time, I bee-line for a rectangular, Barbie-sized box. I tear off the paper to reveal a doll inside. But she's a brunette with a plain blue dress and a cloth on her head. The box says: "Mother Mary." I swallow the lump in my throat.

4. WISHFULNESS

As the storm rages and the rain pours, the children sing "Rain, Rain Go Away." They dream of sunny days, of rainbow-colored sidewalk chalk, plastic slides, and cherry popsicles. They dream of swimming pools, of ice cream trucks' melodies, of sandbox castles. They dream as they sit on tiny chairs pulled up to the window, noses pressed against the glass.

I'm nine, sitting on my grandparents' cement porch with a small knife and two buckets, one with green beans freshly picked from their garden—the other with green beans already de-stringed. While my hands make quick work of the beans, cutting off the ends, pulling out the strings and transferring beans to the other bucket—I dream of success: owning a garage, especially with two stalls, a refrigerator that makes ice, a dress from J.C. Penney's at full price, ordering Coke at a restaurant, Cap'n Crunch cereal, American Girl dolls, Barbie houses, new tennis shoes, anything not handed down, riding an escalator, six-story buildings, light-up billboards, a store I heard about called Macy's.

I accidentally prick my finger with the knife, suck away the blood, then continue.

Success: living in a city, nearby a city, driving to a city, visiting, touring, vacationing, living in something called a city. I'll be a famous movie star when grown-up me lives there; I'll own a purse-sized chihuahua with his own ice maker in our two-stall garage.

These early core memories visit me often, bathing me with their rain. How do these thunderstorms affect the weather forecast for the rest of my life?

Following the Fiddler

At the old-time music festival in the heart of Appalachia, my father, a tall, blue-eyed man with large calloused hands, greets customers with a firm handshake and a smile as they browse the violins normally stored in our basement. A shy ten-year-old girl, I gaze up at the strangers, eyes wide. The women wear turquoise jewelry and long flowy skirts. The men adorned with fringed vests, bolo ties and old-fashioned hats, smelling of sweet cigars. They feel both welcoming and unfamiliar.

Impromptu jam sessions form as one festival-goer starts a folksy tune on the fiddle, a second joins in harmony, a third on mandolin, a fourth tapping spoons on her knee—they follow the lead fiddler, swept up in the music for hours. The teenagers play alongside their grandfathers, toddlers dancing at their feet. In my family, my father represents the lead fiddler and we—my mother, sister, and I—are entangled in the swirling harmonies for as long as he keeps playing.

My father stands on his feet all day, talking to customers. Several purchase resin, bows, or cases, but no instrument sales. As we are packing up at the end, a gray-haired man with a beard visits my father's table and plays a violin that my father had on display. After playing a lively tune, the man returns the fiddle to my father. They barter back and forth over the price, but the man still shakes his head, strokes his beard. My father places the violin back in its case, closes it, hands the man his business card and says, "Well, you know where to find me if you change your mind."

"Wait, wait . . . I'll take it!" The man reaches out and grabs it from my father's arms, then reaches into his pocket for his wallet. I smile. The sale of that violin means hundreds of dollars for our family.

On the ride home, I say, "I didn't think that man was going to buy the violin."

"Yeah, I knew if I packed it up that he would buy it. Sometimes you have to play the game."

I nod my head, thinking my father is the wisest, most business-savvy man in the world. I'm happy to tap a spoon on my knee to the beat of his fiddle's melody.

In the years to come, Dad will quit his day job as an orchestra teacher, try working for his friend's start-up, try working at a chop shop, try selling vacation rentals, try becoming an insurance salesman, a financial advisor, try inventing, try day trading, remain jobless or under-employed for the majority of my growing-up years, insisting that we trust that God will provide and continue to follow his fiddle's ever-changing melody.

But I don't know any of that yet. I smile at my father, drift off to the whirling engine, the fiddle music playing in my head.

My Hillbilly Baptism

Shaking beneath the pastel sky and shy June sun, I'm eleven, wading in cold water up to my belly button, wearing an orange swimsuit and goosebumps. The smell of chlorine, cut grass, and dewy earth fills my nostrils. I bite my lip, look at the small crowd gathered around the reflective water. Their eyes are on me as I tuck a loose strand of hair behind my ear.

The twenty people surrounding me are all members of our "Amen"-saying, tongues-speaking, holy-rolling, driving-out-the-devil church from the hills of West Virginia. We're here, around Pastor's backyard pool, for a baptism ceremony. Pastor, balding with glasses and kind eyes, leads our forty-person non-denominational church however he sees fit. Today, that means I'm to be baptized in his pool, surrounded by my family, fellow saints, and a red-and-white-striped privacy fence.

Mom stands at the edge of the pool, smiling and holding my turquoise towel. Daddy and Pastor wade in the clear blue water, place their large hands upon my head, along the small of my back, guiding me deeper into the water.

I take a deep breath, close my eyes, feel water pruning the lower half of me as I wait and think about what my baptism means to me. I feel God—his hand on my soul, as real as my father's on my back.

Pastor says a quick prayer: *Lord, thank you for send-*

ing your son to die on the cross. Jesus paid the price for our sins, so that we could have a relationship with you and share in eternal life. Bless those who have made the decision to be baptized today. In Jesus' name. Amen.

"Amen" from the crowd. The twenty flock who have gathered hold my gaze, feel the electricity of my moment. My beliefs wait to be wrapped around me with my favorite towel.

We baptize you in the name of the Father, the Son, and the Holy Spirit.

With one dip, one muscular extension—my immersion. I emerge above the surface, grinning and punching my fist toward the sky, dripping with chlorinated water and adolescent faith.

Ten minutes later, half a dozen children in neon swimsuits go screaming, squealing, splashing into the "baptism chamber," and Pastor turns on the grill to cook the hot dogs.

Backpacking

I'm thirteen, fair skinned and gangly, my light brown hair pulled back into a ponytail, sporting a blue hiking backpack and sunglasses—on my first backpacking trip into the Dolly Sods Wilderness in the Monongahela National Forest. There are ten of us—seven teenagers and three adult chaperones.

We had the choice between the hike or writing a book report. I'm not sure why I decided to go. I'm a risk-averse nerd and prefer to experience things from the safety of my favorite reading spot—curled up on our paisley love seat in our small, fireplace-heated living room. But I suppose curiosity fueled my bravery.

We prepared for months for our three-day hike. We bought our tents, hiking boots, thick socks, mole skin, first aid kits, and backpacks. We packed our bags and marched around our middle school's cafeteria, the weight unfamiliar to our tender shoulders. We studied the types of flora and fauna we might encounter—the flowering mountain laurel, a bright orange eastern newt, a black-throated blue warbler—the possibilities seemed exotic, colorful, mysterious.

But nothing prepared me for this—the intensity of the climb, the soreness of my calves and shoulders, and the painful blisters on my toes and heels. But even more so—the jaw-dropping beauty of the high, rocky plateau with its expansive vistas, offering a bird's-eye view of stunted trees, grassy meadows, and wind-carved boulders. I've never seen anything so wondrous, magical.

Our first day, we hike up and up and up, wind through a narrow path, trip over rocks, sweat through our sunscreen and socks. Finally, we stumble upon a clearing. A babbling brook gurgles over small boulders and tree branches. We take off our shoes and socks and wade in the cool water, leaping after crawdads and catching them in our palms, sticking them in each other's faces, giggling.

On the second night of our trip, as we decide on a spot to set up camp, raindrops begin falling on our cheeks. We set up our tents while the rain intensifies, beats down on us with the ferocity of Noah's flood. The three of us girls on the trip huddle in one tent under our sleeping bags, wet, shivering. Usually we would gossip about crushes and first kisses, but now we are quiet, listening to the elephants stomping above our heads.

Mrs. Sloan, our chaperone, pokes her head into the tent and tells us that when the worst of the storm passes, we will head out tonight, cutting our trip short.

When the rain lessens, we pack up and hike down, down, down in the dark. We use flashlights to navigate one muddy step in front of the other. A couple miles into our descent, I slip off of a large log and land on my back with a *thud*. The weight of my pack keeps me belly-up like an overturned tortoise. "I'm just going to lie here for a minute," I say, breathing deeply, looking up at the celestial lights, letting the raindrops pool on my eyelashes and the corners of my eyes.

We make our way, reluctantly, back into the world of streetlights, flushing toilets, and shopping malls. When I fall asleep that night, I dream of colorful flowers, waterfalls, and worlds yet to be explored.

A New World

I'm sitting by myself on the bleachers in the gym. I scan the roaring crowd of several hundred middle schoolers talking, laughing, hugging binders to their chests or flicking paper footballs. My first day of eighth grade, my first time attending a public school. My dad quit his job, so my parents can no longer afford to send me and my sister to the Christian academy we had attended since preschool. I've never seen so many kids my own age. My heart gallops as I wait for the bell. I fidget with my red mesh backpack, zipping and unzipping.

"Fuck!" says the guy sitting behind me. I jump, then try to relax, act normal. "Fuck that shit!" he says. I sneak a look behind me. The guy's jeans hang low, red boxers exposed, and a gold chain hangs around his neck. I try not to stare.

Here, some students don't have hot water, their body odor announcing their presence. Others toss around the N-word like a Hacky Sack. Fights break out almost weekly and drug searches sporadically.

I could adapt, explore this new world—curse a little, try some cigarettes, make out with boys under the bleachers. Instead, I will take advanced classes, escape into novels, and cling to my upbringing like a blankie.

Dear God, What's Beyond These Mountains?

Pastor preaches that you have a plan for my fourteen-year-old life. Can you send it FedEx or angel-bare-back-on-a-horse? What's beyond these cracked sidewalks and dreams crumpled like left-behind clothes post-rapture? Am I to wear the black dust that settled on my grandparents' graves? Can my ancestors' sweat be a soup that fills my belly and fuels the stirring in my soul? Is this home a place around me or a place inside me? And what if I don't like the path you've carved for me, God? What if Pastor is wrong?

Not Her Fault

I'm seventeen. Today is my first day at a three-week academic camp for high school seniors held on a remote college campus in West Virginia. I slide into a seat in the first row of a tiered classroom, beaming at the bald professor as my classmates find their seats. At Professor's bidding, we introduce ourselves. A muscular guy with steel-blue eyes and buzzed hair introduces himself as "Zeke."

"And what's an interesting fact about you, Zeke?" Professor asks.

"I'm a volunteer firefighter, started serving when I turned eighteen," he says.

He says more, but I'm busy tracing his biceps with my eyes, watching the way his lips move.

When it's my turn I say, "Hey everyone, I'm Bethany. My interesting fact is that I have performed as a mime."

Zeke raises his eyebrows, smiles with straight teeth.

It's week two. After breakfast, Zeke and I walk to class holding hands, then sit next to each other for today's lecture. After class, we relax under some shade trees on the lawn. I rest my head on his stomach. Every time he laughs, I feel his abs tighten, bouncing my head up and down, causing my own giggles to rise up like popcorn. We discuss college, careers, politics—anything but us, what we are, how we feel about each other. I sit up and point to pink blossoms on a rhododendron bush nearby—"We have some of those in our yard at home. Aren't they beautiful?"

"Yes," he says, pulling me in for a quick kiss, our first.

After I've resettled on his stomach, Zeke slips his hand up my shirt. The intrusion is as unwanted as a tarantula on my skin. My eyes widen, face flaming, as I glance side to side. The chatting teenagers walking past don't notice. I don't know what to do, so I do nothing.

The next day, Professor leads us out of our classroom and down the hallway to a corner full of oversized bean bags. We slowly sink into the bean bags, our bodies half enveloped. Zeke's legs rub against mine. As Professor lectures, Zeke creeps his fingers up my leg, over my thigh, into my loose-fitting shorts. Adrenaline shouts in my veins. *What is he doing? We've barely kissed. I should've smacked him away yesterday. This is my fault. What am I supposed to do? I don't want to make a scene. Stay quiet.*

I silently will Professor to notice and intervene. He doesn't. I sit frozen, pretending to focus on the lecture while Zeke's fingers discover parts of me no man has ever touched before. After eternity-long seconds, I push Zeke's hand away.

After class I try to shrug off the sickening feeling in my gut. *This means Zeke wants to get serious with me. He must really like me,* I think as I walk back to my dorm room, flicking my hair behind me.

The next day, after breakfast, I wait for Zeke. He walks

past me conversing with a girl with perfect skin and a tiny waist. He doesn't make eye contact, doesn't glance in my direction. I swallow the lump in my throat and instinctively suck in my stomach.

On our last night of camp, the lunchroom is transformed into a dance floor. The bass vibrates my heart as I shout "I'll miss you" and "Where do you live again?" to friends in between the "Chicken Dance" and the "Cha Cha Slide." Zeke grinds with the other girl, moving his hands up and down her body while the jewel-like disco ball lights swirl around them. My stomach churns. I'm grateful he isn't groping me, but part of me still wishes he would kiss me again, stroke my hair, whisper in my ear.

This whole thing is my fault. I'm such a screw-up when it comes to boys. I leave the dance floor, get a drink of water, slip out into the cool evening air—unaware that in the future, as a mother, I'll revisit this memory, take my teenage self into my motherly arms and tell her, "It was not your fault, child. It was NOT your fault."

Out-of-State College

The question arrives with the new notebooks, shiny laptops, and friendly faces in the dorm, cafeteria, library, at the churches that I visit: *Where are you from?*

I answer, smiling.

Some kind responses. Some smug faces, spitting words: *Kissin' cousins, right? You actually own shoes? Wow, you have all your teeth too.*

Still smiling—on the outside.

Dr. Edwards, history professor, lectures: *West Virginia—the most illegitimate state. Mountaineers didn't ask, didn't wait, just split, statehood signed by over-eager Abe.* A statehood identity crisis: southernmost North or northernmost South or maybe Mid-Atlantic.

Leaning forward in the front row, I twirl my pen—my heart torn over whether to claim the illegitimate as my own.

When a new face asks the same question, I consider lying. Instead I swallow my shame and whisper, "West Virginia."

Torn

Away from my West Virginia home, as a college student in Pennsylvania, I unpack my suitcase of ambition, duffel bag of nerves, and pour myself into my studies and campus activities. Weeks have gone by since I talked to my parents. My mom texts: "Your dad is sad you don't call." I call, phone tucked under my ear as I carry my laundry down the hall to the dorm laundry room. "I'm busy. Two exams, a sorority event, and I'm running for president of an honor society," I tell my mom, cutting the call short.

While I distance myself from my parents, I become obsessed with Appalachia in my studies. My history paper is "Black Lungs and Rednecks: Life in the Coal Towns." For a research methods class, I examine "Regional Identity: A Study of Appalachian English." For rhetorical studies, I analyze Obama's memorial service address for the Upper Branch Coal Miners. For my creative writing class, I write an essay entitled "Home: Jail or Safehouse?" and a poem: "When I Say I'm from West Virginia." I can't read enough, write enough, soak in enough about my culture, home, and identity—all while rolling my eyes at my parents' text messages and not speaking to my sister or grandparents for months.

In between classes, alone in my dorm room, I get a call from my dad. My dad never calls. "Hello?" I answer.

"Bethany, your grandfather passed away this morning."

"Oh, I'm so sorry, Dad." I place my left hand on my heart, watch the rain pitter-pattering on the leaves outside my window.

We talk in hushed voices for a short while, then I say, "I have to go. My philosophy class starts in fifteen minutes." I pull on my polka-dotted rain boots and walk across campus, letting the raindrops hit my cheeks in place of tears—unable to process that I've lost someone I love.

My parents and I decide I won't be going home for the funeral. Although home is only a two-and-a-half-hour drive away, I don't have a car. Mom doesn't drive long distances, and Dad doesn't have the time or emotional energy to make the trip on the same weekend he has to bury his father. When we make the decision, I feel relieved. I have a busy weekend of studying and hanging out with friends planned.

On Saturday morning, the day of the funeral, I roll out of bed, check the time on my phone. My grandfather's funeral is about to begin, and I'm not there. I feel like I'm drowning. I sink into my mattress and pull the covers over my head.

Afterward, I try to call home more often, but my studies and friends are all-consuming. I sign up for an independent study. My research proposal: "A mission for the Mountain State: exploring poverty and obesity in the eyes of West Virginia's youth." For a scholarship application, I write: "Whether through serving the people of Appalachia, being their spokesperson, writing their stories, or just through research I know that I want to live and work in West Virginia." And yet whenever I visit home, I'm reminded of my less-than-pleasant school experiences and that neither of my parents have jobs. Things that once felt normal to me, I now see as signs of poverty—cars with rust, a large percentage of obese people, the way both people and buildings tend to deteriorate instead of flourish.

Before my senior year of college, I land an internship at a publishing company in Morgantown, West Virginia. I love writing for their regional lifestyle magazines. This is what I'm going to do for the rest of my life, I think. I'm going to write about and celebrate West Virginia. But they only pay their entry-level writers twelve dollars an hour, and housing in Morgantown (home to West Virginia University) is expensive. So senior year, when I apply for jobs, I don't apply for any in West Virginia. I can't find any opportunities there that align with my desire to write and to live on my own. Instead, I apply for jobs all over the country, particularly in Pennsylvania near my college.

I receive an offer from a marketing agency in Pittsburgh to be a creative copywriter. I'm thrilled. My dream job—writing, living in a city, living on my own. "It's perfect," I tell friends and family, forgetting that just a few months prior I believed West Virginia was calling me home.

I pack up my suitcase of ambition, duffel bag of nerves, set out for the city. A fresh start. It's good to leave my past behind. Yes, it's a good thing, I tell myself in my travel-size mirror.

First Night in City Apartment

My nocturnal symphony—cricket cellists, owls on bassoons, raccoon's racket, dogs baying at the moon, creek gurgles, bonfire crackles—vanished, evaporated, or drowned. Instead: heavy footsteps, doors shuttering, engines barking, horns yelling, brakes hissing, sirens whistling, voices dancing, rap music rattling, and the clank-and-crash of trash tossed into the bin.

The cacophony finally lessens; I nestle in. Until the upstairs neighbors start a rhythmic love-making session above my head. I lie in bed, hugging knees to chest—for the first time, but not the last time—violently alone, missing home.

Dirt-Road Dress Shopping

In the middle of West Virginia, my parents and I follow a bumpy dirt road past a run-down trailer and fields of raspberries to a large white building with a sign—"Dinah's Boutique." Twenty minutes later, in the shower curtain-enclosed dressing room, I step into a lacy white gown.

I know right away I'm buying this wedding dress, never mind that I've only tried on three dresses, that this is the first dress shop I've visited, that these long, puffy sleeves look ridiculous. It hugs my curves, and it's cheap.

I'm twenty-four, two years out of college, working a marketing job in Pittsburgh. I make enough to buy a more expensive dress, but my parents insist on paying for it. They barely have any income, but they scraped together a little money for my wedding. I'll be damned if I spend it all on a dress that I'll wear once.

So when Mom says, "Well, what do you think?" as I'm standing on the stool in front of the semicircle of mirrors, I say, despite the sagging sleeves, "It fits perfectly."

"It looks great on you. Really makes you look thin."

"Mmhmm." I bite my tongue so as not to say something about how being thin isn't my goal. "I think it's the one. I may get the sleeves removed, but that's an easy fix."

"Oh, you don't like the sleeves?" Mom wrinkles her forehead, pulls on the sleeves of her paisley-print T-shirt she scored for fifty cents at a yard sale.

"Not sure. But like I said, it's easy for a seamstress to remove them."

I wish I could remove feelings from my past like these God-awful sleeves. Remove the feelings of not having enough, of not being enough. Live only in the present, gliding toward my future with a sail as white as this dress.

"What do you think, honey?" Mom says to Dad; his large, over-worn, white-turned-gray tennis shoes are strange visitors in this land of silver stilettos.

"It's nice," he nods, eyes on me. "You look beautiful."

I smile. My dad would think I look beautiful in anything. I wish my bridesmaids were here to give me their opinions, but the time and location of this trip didn't allow them to come. When Mom and Dad wanted to go today, while I'm in West Virginia visiting them, I agreed, like I always do.

My need to make my parents happy—that will change once I'm married, right? I know I shouldn't care what they think. I'm an adult, after all. But I can't stand the thought of disappointing them. It's why in high school I pushed myself to become valedictorian. They beamed at me when I gave my speech. Mom had a tear running down her cheek. It's a good thing though—it earned me scholarships for college. They couldn't have afforded to send me otherwise.

I'm looking forward to that too—being able to afford things. My fiancé and I, once we combine our incomes, will make significantly more than what my parents have lived on for the last decade. It will be nice strolling into a department store to buy a sweater, instead of combing the clearance rack for 80%-off deals.

"Oh, don't you just look lovely." A saleswoman circles me, inspecting my body with her eyes.

I force a smile.

"Would you like to try a veil?"

"Oh, I don't know if I really want one," I mumble.

"Oh, you will once you try one on, trust me."

She grabs a fake-pearl-lined veil and places it on my head. The veil is beautiful, but aren't veils kind of old-fashioned? Do brides even wear them anymore?

My parents smile wide at me; Mom tears up again.

"How much is it?" Mom asks.

"Oh, this one is only twenty dollars. You won't find a veil anywhere else for that price."

"We'll take it!" Dad says.

"I—" I say.

I'll be their little girl for a little while longer, tagging along this bumpy ride. But once I'm married, I'll create my own smoothly paved path. At least, I'm going to try.

Roots

I'd left it all behind—the neighbors' sun-faded trailer and asbestos-filled house with broken-teeth windows at the entrance to our dead-end street; the man with a pit-stained tank top, cigarette hanging from the corner of his lips, cat purring around his legs; the dogs, one or two in each yard—barking, howling, whining; the rusted cars, smell of burning wood, sounds of distant gunshots in the woods; hills so steep you can scrape the bottom of your car on the cracked asphalt; neighbors who know when your mail piles up, lawn mower breaks, when you're sunbathing or laughing or fighting with your sister over a borrowed sweater found balled up beneath your bed; the way the houses start to peel or grow moss or lose their shutters; the Appalachian Mountains as both beautiful backdrop and formidable, omniscient jailers.

I'd left it all behind at eighteen when I accumulated enough scholarships to attend an out-of-state college, a few hours north, a state away, far enough to feel like I'd escaped. I've visited my parents a few times each year, but each time with a rubber-band ball of dread tightening my gut, constricting up my throat with each pothole I hit or swerve to avoid.

I'm thirty with a family of my own; we're visiting my parents for the July 4th holiday. The next town over—Stonewood, West Virginia, where my mother grew up and where I was born—is celebrating its seventy-fifth anniversary with a festival. We're at the festival, sitting at folding tables inside the local fire station—me, my husband, and our two-year-old son slurping on a purple snow cone. My mother is nearby chatting with someone.

"Bethany, I want you to meet Mary Lou. I taught with her at Norwood." Mom leads an older woman over toward me.

Mary Lou, eighty-eight, wears glasses, sunspots, makeup creased around her mouth. She smiles wide as she talks, standing closer to me than I'm used to.

"You know, I went to Norwood from first through ninth grade. Then I taught there for thirty years. And I didn't even go to college until after my kids were in grade school. When I went to Fairmont for college it was ninety-nine dollars per semester!"

"Wow!" I realize she's lived her entire life in this tiny town.

We chat about her children, grandchildren, community activities. She tells us she has her thirteen great-grandkids over every Sunday for dinner. I feel a few of those rubber bands in my gut loosening.

"I see her out and about all the time," my mom tells me after Mary Lou leaves. "She's almost ninety, but she doesn't let that stop her. She always says, 'The Lord has been good to me.' She's volunteering here cleaning off the tables all day; bless her heart."

More rubber bands dissolve.

As we explore the festival, the smell of pepperoni rolls and kettle corn hangs in the humid air, clings to our clothes and the sweat under our arms. In my suburban, near-city life, I'm accustomed to seas of unfamiliar faces. Here, my mother stops to greet an acquaintance or friend every ten feet, getting pulled into conversations, greeted with handshakes or hugs.

My son sees a booth selling cake and cookies. "Cake. I want cake!" He runs over and reaches toward the table.

"No, no. We're not buying cake," I say.

One of the young men who is working the booth says, "Would he like a cookie?" and pulls out a bag of peanut butter cookies. "Here, reach your hand in there and grab one. You can have it for free. It's our snack."

My son reaches his hand in and grabs two.

"Oh sure, you can have two." The man smiles.

I thank him, feel the ball in my gut shrinking to the size of a marble.

During the rest of the weekend, we splash in a blow-up pool, hang out on a deck with neighbors and sip flavored water, swing on the porch swing, read books, sit in the sun, discuss theology with my dad late into the night, light sparklers.

On our way home, the ball of dread is gone. I turn to my husband and say, "Something was different this time. I don't feel the angst that I used to feel when I went back home."

Home—I hadn't thought about it like that for years.

Porch-sitting; pepperoni rolls, hoagies, hot dogs with chili sauce, blackberry cobblers with vanilla ice cream, apple juice popsicles; scriptures on the walls, a Bible in every room; neighbors who watch you grow, strangers who offer cookies, share stories; fireflies and firepits and fireworks; bare toes in mossy grass, sunshine and shade and splashing in the creek; folksy fiddle music that plays between my ears long after the musicians are gone; ten dollars in my pocket for a festival meal; the earthy smell after a rain, earthworms emerging from warm soil, robins feasting; being known by a place and the people of that place, feeling that place reverberating in your chest, soaking into your pores, pickling your heart; growing deep roots—I'd left it all behind.

Acknowledgments

I'm grateful to the following journals for publishing these essays, often in different forms: "Yellow" was published as "Definition: The Color Between Green and Orange" in *Harpy Hybrid*. "A New World" and part of "Big Feelings, Little Self" was published as "Fundamentally Flawed" in *Rougarou Journal*. "My Hillbilly Baptism" was published as "Wade in the Water" in *Heart of Flesh*. "Backpacking" was published as "Mountain Rain" in *Deep Wild Journal*. "Dear God, What's Beyond These Mountains?" was published in *Still: The Journal*. "First Night in City Apartment" was published in *Underscore Magazine*. "Roots" was published in *Flyover Country*.

"A Note on Truth" is adapted from Maryanne Aita's "A Note on Truth" at the beginning of her memoir *Little Astronaut: A Memoir in Essays* (ELJ Editions, 2022), and is used with her permission.

I'm grateful to the members of two writing groups who gave me invaluable feedback and emotional support as I wrote this chapbook. Thank you to my long-time writing group members: Sarah Abbott, Victoria Zeolla, Wendi Kozma, and Karla Fossett. Thank you also to my CNF writing group (I miss you!): Eileen Finley, Debbie Chase, Linda Jones, and Carol Raitt.

I also want to thank Chelsey Clammer who provided excellent editing and feedback on an earlier draft.

An enormous thank you to Belle Point Press and Casie Dodd for believing in my work, selecting my manuscript for publication, and for making my book-dreams come true.

A special thank you to my high school English teacher, Ms. Terri Boggs, for believing in me and giving me the tools I needed as a fledgling writer.

I'd also like to thank my parents for teaching me to love books and encouraging me in my writing when I was young and for giving me their "blessing" to publish this chapbook.

A special thank you to my husband who has always been my number one fan.

Finally, I'm thankful to God, from whom all blessings flow.

Bethany Jarmul is an Appalachian writer and poet. She's the author of two chapbooks, and her debut poetry collection *Lightning Is a Mother* is forthcoming with ELJ Editions in 2025. Her work was selected for *Best Spiritual Literature 2023* and *Best Small Fictions 2024*, and has been nominated for the *Pushcart Prize*, *Best of the Net*, *Best Microfiction*, and *Wigleaf* Top 50. Connect with her at bethanyjarmul.com or on social media: @BethanyJarmul.

BELLE
POINT
PRESS